STAG LINE
and
JOSEPH ROBINSON
AND SONS

by
Nicholas J. Robinson

Published by the World Ship Society
Kendal LA9 7LT
1984

 Red

The Company house flag and funnel mark consist of a red background and a white stag trippant. Originally, this was a heraldic stag but from 1948 a more realistic looking stag was designed, using one of the stags heads which adorned the private office.

A stag trippant was the crest of several North Country Robinson families, so also was the motto "Virtute Non Verbis", but we have not been able to find a record of a stag trippant combined with this motto. Nor have we been able to trace any direct family link to the Heralds Visitations of Yorkshire in 1612 and 1666.

The first use of the word "stag" was when Captain Joseph Robinson used this name for his first newly built ship in 1846. The fact that he chose this name indicates that he had some connection with the family crest. This connection is further confirmed in a painting dated 1867 of the barque "Eleanor Grace" (built 1849) which shows a red house flag with a white heraldic stag trippant on it. This was further confirmed on the painting of the first steamer "Stephanotis" (built 1871) which vessel, in addition to the stag house flag, had a stag on the funnel. The funnel was black with a red band and white stag trippant on it.

1 HOWARD STREET, NORTH SHIELDS, BUILT 1807 *Author's Collection*

THE HOME OF STAG LINE
FOR NINETY YEARS

A BRIEF HISTORY OF THE STAG LINE

The Founder, James Robinson, was born in the North Yorkshire port of Whitby in 1768. He was the son of a sailor and, like his father, he also took to the sea and in due course became 1st. Mate on a Whitby vessel. In 1796, however, he signed off in London and moved to North Shields where he settled and in the following year married a Northumbrian girl. Of their eight children, two were to take up seafaring careers and thus maintain a family tradition. It was some time however, before the Robinson family were to acquire a vessel of their own. This opportunity came when there was a reduction in the demand for shipping and a consequent drop in the value of ships at the end of the Napoleonic wars. In 1817 Captain James Robinson took his chance to buy the brig BLESSING of 221 tons, which had been built at Sunderland twelve years previously, in the year of Trafalgar.

In the late 1820's a further recession in trade caused him to raise money by a loan against the ship. James Robinson died in 1833 and the management of the BLESSING passed to his wife Grace. Their sons, Captain John and Captain Joseph Robinson commanded the BLESSING from time to time. In 1843 Joseph (always known as Captain Joseph) took over the loan and when his mother Grace died in the following year he became sole owner of the ship.

In March 1846 the BLESSING was lost and it would appear that Joseph, using the insurance money, ordered a new vessel from Luke, Blumer and Bushell of South Shields and named her STAG. The prevalent method of shipowning was to divide the ownership into 64 shares, known as the 64ther system. Of the 64 shares in the STAG, Joseph took 28, his brother Thomas, a tailor, took 22 and James Miller, a previous employer, took 14 shares. A stag trippant is the crest of a North Yorkshire branch of the Robinson family and was adopted as the house flag. "Trippant" is a heraldic term where an animal has one foot raised in a trotting action.

Over the next quarter century the demand for shipping expanded due to the Industrial Revolution, the increase in the population of the United Kingdom and the importation of foreign grain due to the repealing of the Corn Laws. This gave Joseph the right conditions to increase the fleet and in 1848 the FELLOWSHIP was purchased secondhand but was sold in the following year and replaced by the newly-built ELEANOR GRACE. A painting shows her flying a Stag flag on her main mast. She was followed in 1853 with the purchase of the eleven year old ALBERT and in 1856 the ROBINSONS was completed at Sunderland. From 1850 onwards the fleet was managed by Joseph Robinson and Company. Joseph owned a large portion of the 64th. shares in each ship whilst other shares were owned by his relations, local traders and professional men. The first ship with a flower name was the barque CAMELLIA, built in 1858. By 1871 Joseph had built up a fleet of one brig and eight barques totalling 3,282 tons in all.

The development of the compound steam engine in 1852 and the opening of the Suez Canal in 1869 persuaded many British shipowners to change from sail to steam. In 1871 the STEPHANOTIS was the Company's first steam ship and, carrying a stag on her funnel, was delivered by Iliff, Mounsey and Company of Sunderland. In addition to sails she had a 98 h.p. steam engine and was of 1,042 tons gross. Eight years later there were no sailing ships left in the fleet which then consisted of eleven steamers of 16,113 tons.

In October 1880 the Company had the misfortune to lose two vessels in unusual circumstances. The steamers STAG and ROBINIA, both on passage from New Orleans to French ports, were at anchor at Punta Delgada, Azores. During a severe storm the anchors of both vessels dragged and the two ships collided. The anchors of the British steamer BENELLA also failed to hold and she collided with the ROBINIA. When the storm had passed the three ships were to be seen lying wrecked in the harbour.

The management firm of Joseph Robinson and Company was changed to Joseph Robinson and Sons in 1883 after three sons had joined the partnership. In 1889 Captain Joseph Robinson died, having seen the fleet grow to sixteen steamers of 28,302 tons. He was typical of those hard-working, thrusting Victorians who built up the nineteenth century prosperity of Britain. In 1891 Joseph Robinson and Sons moved its office to No. 1 Howard Street, North Shields which was to be its home for ninety years. The building had been erected as the first Subscription Library in the North of England, the foundation stone being laid in 1806.

In 1895, due to the high cost of insuring each ship individually on the market, it was arranged with all the 64th shareholders to transfer the ships to a limited company known as "Stag Line", Ltd. which would carry its own insurance. Of the shares in the new company 72% were held by the family with the balance being held by friends and local traders. Joseph Robinson and Sons continued as managers and also acted as directors of the limited company. "Stag Line", Ltd. was established with a paid up capital of £148,032 divided into 16,448 shares of £9. In a letter dated 11th December 1895, Joseph Robinson and Sons explained how the transfer would be effected.

Name of Ship	(1)	(2)	(3)	Date of Transfer
STEPHANOTIS	£4,608	512	8	2nd September 1895
CAMELLIA	£6,912	768	12	2nd September 1895
VIOLA	£9,216	1,024	16	4th September 1895
CORONILLA	£6,912	768	12	16th September 1895
GLADIOLUS	£10,368	1,152	18	18th September 1895
EGLANTINE	£6,912	768	12	27th September 1895
AMARYLLIS	£6,912	768	12	30th September 1895
ROBINIA	£13,248	1,472	23	30th September 1895
GARDENIA	£9,216	1,024	16	2nd October 1895
STAG	£13,248	1,472	23	2nd October 1895
LAURESTINA	£13,248	1,472	23	5th October 1895
IXIA	£10,944	1,216	19	14th October 1895
CYDONIA	£6,912	768	12	19th October 1895
CLINTONIA	£10,944	1,216	19	24th October 1895
AZALEA	£7,488	832	13	26th October 1895
NYMPHAEA	£10,944	1,216	19	11th December 1895

Paid up Capital   £148,032 =16,448 shares at £9

Notes: (1). Value of the steamer on transfer to "Stag Line", Ltd.
        (2). Number of £9 shares in "Stag Line", Ltd. allocated in respect of each vessel. (Value of the steamer divided by £9).
        (3). Number of £9 shares in "Stag Line", Ltd. allocated in exchange for each former 64th. share in the ship. (Column (2) divided by 64).

In 1896, with shipbuilders quoting keen prices, the first order for 13 years was placed for a steamer with triple expansion engines and 4,310 tons carrying capacity at a cost of £27,860. This compared with £31,250 paid for the STAG of 2,900 tons and built in 1884. The new ship was completed in January 1897 as GLOXINIA and marked the beginning of a policy to sell the

GLOXINIA   *G. Scott Collection*

older ships and replace them with larger and more modern vessels. Three more steamers followed during the next three years and continued the long association with the Tyne Iron Shipbuilding Co. Ltd. who delivered two more ships in 1904. By 1904 two brothers and a cousin of the fourth generation of Robinsons were at the helm with a fleet of ten ships of 29,414 tons. In the same year, with a more encouraging freight market, orders were placed for two Doxford turret steamers of 6,600 tons. These two ships were completed in 1907 as EUPHORBIA and CLINTONIA. The policy of replacing ships continued whilst some of the older vessels were fitted for the carriage of molasses in bulk.

When the War broke out in 1914 the Company had a fleet of twelve steamers with a carrying capacity of 65,460 tons. Seven ships were lost during the conflict including the EUPHORBIA completed in 1917 and the BEGONIA built in 1918.

In order to replace war losses and older less efficient ships that had been sold, the managers in 1916 obtained permission from the shareholders to build six new steamers but due to Government restrictions on the building of ships for private investment it was only possible to build limited replacement tonnage.

When the War ended in 1918 the Company had only two ships, the GARDENIA of 1914 and the CLINTONIA of 1917, with an order for a third ship deferred due to Government restrictions.

As there was little prospect of building new ships for some time, it was decided to reconstitute the Company and distribute surplus cash to the

7

shareholders. The new company, named Stag Line, Ltd. was registered on the 26th August 1918 with two ships totalling 10,700 tons deadweight. The Company returned to the Tyne Iron Shipbuilding Co. Ltd. for the first ship of the post-war building programme. She was, however, to be the last ship to be built at the yard for Stag Line and marked the end of a long association between owner and builder. The GLOXINIA was completed as a cargo steamer in September 1920 but was immediately handed over to Smith's Dock Co. Ltd. at North Shields and converted into a tanker.

IXIA wrecked on the Cornish coast   *F. E. Gibson*

The IXIA joined the fleet in July 1922 and served the Company until 30th June 1929 when she was wrecked on The Brisons. The loss of the IXIA had far-reaching effects and became the leading case, decided by the House of Lords, on the complicated subject of reasonable deviation of course. The IXIA was fitted with a superheater and when she sailed from Swansea on passage to Constantinople with a cargo of coal there were two shore engineers on board for the purpose of observing the working of the superheater at the beginning of the voyage. The two engineers were subsequently transferred from the ship in St. Ives Bay by a boat which put out from the shore. In order to effect this transfer, the vessel deviated some five miles off the normal course for the Mediterranean so as to enter St. Ives Bay. Thereafter the IXIA kept closer to the Cornish coast than if she had been on the normal course. Shortly afterwards she ran aground and was lost with her cargo, though the weather conditions were fairly good at the time. The charterers claimed the full value of the cargo from the shipowners. The Company maintained that a clause in the Bill of Lading provided for such a deviation of course but the House of Lords ruled against the Company.

Two ships were delivered by the Sunderland Shipbuilding Co. Ltd. in 1924 and named LINARIA and EUPHORBIA. The next ship to be delivered to the Company was the steamer CYDONIA. The keel of this ship had been laid down at the North Dock yard of J. Blumer and Co. Ltd., Sunderland in 1922.

The hull of the ship stood on the stocks for four years whilst the shipyard was closed. It was not until December 1926 that the vessel was launched after the shipyard had reopened. The ship was purchased by Stag Line and as the CYDONIA she sailed from Sunderland in January 1927. A sistership which had been built in similar circumstances was completed in December 1926 as the USWORTH, having been purchased by the Dalgleish Steam Shipping Co. Ltd., Newcastle. The completion of the CYDONIA however, marked the end of shipbuilding at the North Dock, Sunderland.

CYDONIA *York Collection*

In December 1928 the Company took delivery of the GARDENIA. This ship had been launched as the STRONGARM, having been commenced on speculation by Armstrong, Whitworth and Co. Ltd., Newcastle. The fleet had been built up to six ships totalling 35,173 tons when the slump started in 1930. All the vessels were laid up for extended periods and the tanker GLOXINIA lay idle at Stanhope Buoys in the River Tyne from 14th. October 1930 until 26th January 1937. It was eight years before full depreciation had been provided and it was possible to recommend the payment of dividends again. Despite this however, the bank overdraft never exceeded £4,750.

By September 1939, when the Second World War started, the fleet totalled seven ships, following the purchase in 1938 of a secondhand steamer which was renamed PHOTINIA. On 12th March 1940 the GARDENIA was lost as a result of enemy action, followed by the CLINTONIA and EUPHORBIA later the same year. The LINARIA was torpedoed and sunk on 24th February 1941 and although the Company had lost four ships within twelve months it was fortunate in that no more ships were sunk during the remainder of the war; however, several vessels managed on behalf of the Government were lost.

Although in 1940 the Company had agreed to purchase the steamer HOLLINSIDE 4172/30 from Charlton, McAllum and Co. Ltd., Newcastle and had selected the name BEGONIA for her, a disagreement arose over the condition of the ship and the terms of the final contract and Stag Line withdrew. On the following voyage her stern frame fractured and the HOLLINSIDE had to be towed into Punta Delgada, Azores where she arrived on 16th March 1941. In 1943 the Company purchased the ELIZABETH MASSEY but wartime regulations prevented the renaming of the ship and so it was in 1945 that she took the name BEGONIA. The steamer BRIARWOOD was purchased in 1945 and application was made to change her name to ZINNIA. In fact she was renamed GARDENIA on 13th December 1945.

In 1946 Nicholas Robinson, after serving six years in the Royal Corps of Signals, joined his cousin David as a partner in Joseph Robinson and Sons. Their cousin, Robin Pender, joined the firm in 1954 and became a partner in 1957 to complete the fifth generation team. During the immediate post-war years the Company purchased four war-built steamers. The EMPIRE KUMASI became the IXIA whilst H.M.S. SANCROFT, formerly the EMPIRE BAFFIN, was renamed CLINTONIA. Both the ships had been previously managed by the Company and were converted from coal to oil firing before entering service with Stag Line. H.M.S. MORAY FIRTH had been laid down as EMPIRE PITCAIRN but completed as a maintenance repair ship for the Admiralty whilst H.M.S. PORTLAND BILL had been similarly employed. These two ships, after conversion back to dry cargo carriers, were renamed LINARIA and ZINNIA respectively.

The CYDONIA was one of the ships which survived the war although on 28th February 1945 she had struck a mine in the North Sea and arrived at Hull in a damaged condition. On 21st. October 1949 she again had the misfortune to strike a mine. The ship was on passage from Workington to Cardiff when the mine was seen on the surface about 200 yards away. Avoiding action was taken but owing to the force of the wind she drifted down on to the mine. The engine room flooded rapidly and a greaser on watch lost his life. The remainder of the crew was rescued by the ST. CLEARS 4308/36 of the South American Saint Line Ltd. and the ship was towed to Milford Haven by the tug ENGLISHMAN 762/45. She was found to be badly damaged however, and was sold to be broken up.

CAMELLIA *T. Rayner*

In 1950 the first steps were taken to replace the fleet with modern dry cargo bulk carriers and an order was placed with J. Readhead and Sons Ltd., South Shields. This ship was completed in February 1953 as CAMELLIA and was the first motorship in the fleet. She was followed in 1955 by the steamer CYDONIA from the same yard. During the ice-free season of 1956 the BEGONIA, CAMELLIA, CLINTONIA and GARDENIA each made two voyages to Churchill in Hudson Bay, Canada, and lifted a total of 59,112 tons of grain. This was regarded at the time as a record outloading in one season by one shipping company. The BEGONIA was sold at the end of 1956 and other steamers were also sold as new tonnage was delivered. In May 1958 the motorship GLOXINIA was completed to bring the fleet to six ships.

10

GARDENIA in the Welland Canal

Author's Collection

A notable achievement of the Stag Line management was their quickness off the mark in recognising the importance of the St. Lawrence Seaway, opened in 1959. Before construction had finished, visits were made to Canada and the Great Lakes to discover its potential for deep-sea ships. The CAMELLIA and GARDENIA had the distinction of being the first deep-sea ships to be chartered to load in the Great Lakes when they were fixed on 12th November 1958. The vessels were fitted with equipment for the St. Lawrence Seaway in April 1959 prior to sailing from the River Tyne. They both entered the Seaway on 3rd May 1959, eight days after it had opened to commercial traffic.

In March 1961 the PHOTINIA was completed by J. Readhead and Sons Ltd., South Shields. Just before she was delivered, arrangements had been made to timecharter her to British Insulated Callender's Cable Company to lay three 5″ diameter power cables across Cook Strait between North and South Island, New Zealand. After a few months trading the ship returned to the builder's yard to be fitted with cable laying equipment. On 7th March 1962 she sailed from the River Tyne and carried out laying trials in Loch Fyne before returning to the shipyard at the end of April to have the equipment removed. The PHOTINIA then resumed normal trading until the manufacture of the 75 miles of cable had been completed. In February 1964 the ship arrived at South Shields for the cable laying equipment to be refitted and then proceeded to Loch Fyne for more trials before sailing to Manchester to take on board three 25 mile lengths of 5″ diameter high voltage submarine power cable. The PHOTINIA sailed from Manchester on 22nd August 1964 and successfully completed the laying of the cable in November. After returning to the United Kingdom the ship loaded a further 25 mile length of cable which she laid between Trinidad and Tobago during September 1965. With her cable laying tasks completed, the PHOTINIA returned to the River Tyne where the equipment was landed and she reverted to her normal role as a bulk carrier.

During 1964 the Company sold the last of the pre-war and war built tonnage, and the fleet was strengthened with the delivery of the IXIA by Austin and Pickersgill Ltd., Sunderland. She was the largest ship that the Company had owned up to that time whilst her dimensions and equipment enabled her to trade to the St. Lawrence Seaway. In 1965 the IXIA arrived in the River Mersey with a cargo of 23,192 tons of grain from Canada which, at the time, was the largest bulk grain cargo to be discharged in the river. The

CYDONIA   *Skyfotos*

CYDONIA had the distinction in October 1965 of making the fiftieth voyage to the Seaway by a Stag Line ship when she discharged a cargo of ferro-manganese from Boulogne and loaded a cargo of grain homewards.

The Company placed an order with J. Readhead and Sons Ltd. in 1966 for another bulk carrier and in October 1968 she was completed as ZINNIA. The CYDONIA was the last steamer in the fleet and in August 1969 she was sold to Liberian-flag owners. During 1969 the managing partnership of Joseph Robinson and Sons was absorbed into Stag Line, Ltd. and with an improved freight market the company was in a position to benefit from the trading by its fleet of modern bulk carriers. The motorship CAMELLIA was sold in 1972 and the year closed with the Company operating a fleet of four ships.

Early in 1974 it was announced that Ropner Holdings Ltd. had purchased a shareholding in Stag Line, Ltd. which represented 27.94% of the issued share capital.

The Company acquired two ships in April 1975 for which bareboat charters had been arranged. These vessels were renamed KIELDER STAG and SILLOTH STAG and were engaged in the coastal and short sea trades. In January 1976, following the cancellation of a number of their orders, Swan Hunter Shipbuilders Ltd. submitted an attractive offer to build a third 26,000 ton deadweight bulkcarrier which was named BEGONIA and delivered in May 1978. This was a valuable order for the Tyneside shipyard and was followed later in 1976 with a contract for J. Readhead and Sons Ltd. to refit the PHOTINIA for a further cable laying operation. A fault had developed in one of the Cook Strait cables and so in October 1976 the PHOTINIA commenced conversion prior to making the voyage to New Zealand. On 20th August 1977 the repair was completed and the ship sailed for the River Tyne. She was then once more converted back to her bulk carrier role but, unfortunately, her career ended in May 1978 when she was driven aground by a storm off Milwaukee and was declared a total loss.

Sadly, on 3rd March 1977 David Robinson C.B.E., J.P. died suddenly whilst on business in London. He had retired as chairman of Stag Line in 1975 but had remained on the board. In addition to his association with Stag Line, he had held several other posts and was a past president of the Chamber of Shipping.

The BEGONIA was completed in May 1978 and to finance her the GLOXINIA was sold during 1977 and the KIELDER STAG was sold in the following year. With freight rates at rock bottom and 400 dry cargo ships totalling 13 million tons deadweight laid up, the Company had difficulty in meeting the Government loan repayments. However, the granting of a three year deferment helped the Company through the worst of the depression and with a strong demand for tonnage following the failure of the U.S.S.R. grain harvest, the Company moved back into profitability in 1980. With a second U.S.S.R. grain failure, a forecasted increase in demand for coal to replace a continuing shortage and high cost of oil and with the lowest dry cargo laid up figures since 1975 (just over 2 million tonnes deadweight) the trading prospects for 1981 looked very good.

Early in 1981, Ropner Holdings Ltd. who had bought a total of 29% of the shares in Stag Line in 1974, sold their holding to Hunting Gibson plc. who then made a public offer for all the shares. Stag Line Directors recommended acceptance as this was in the best interests of all concerned and Stag Line, Ltd. became a wholly owned subsidiary of Hunting Gibson on 1st April 1981. Hunting Stag Management Ltd. was set up in Newcastle to absorb the sea going and shore based staff of Hunting and Son and Stag Line, and to manage the Hunting and Stag fleets. Nicholas J. Robinson, however, stayed with Stag Line as non-executive chairman until 31st December 1982. In October 1981 the offices in 1 Howard Street, North Shields, occupied by Stag Line for 90 years, were sold.

Unfortunately, the deepening world recession caused a drop in the demand for raw materials, the U.S.S.R. met much of her demand for grain from Europe's bumper harvest and the delivery of many large bulk carriers ordered during 1980 and 1981 resulted in freight rates starting to fall during 1981. By the end of 1982 the number of dry cargo ships laid up due to lack of employment had reached 1,146 of 24 million tonnes deadweight, 7% of the world dry cargo fleet. Medium sized bulk carriers under the British flag, if trading, were losing around £1,000 a day and shipowning faced a worse situation than during the 1930's depression. To reduce losses the IXIA was sold in February 1982, when 17 years old, for just over her building price. The SILLOTH STAG together with Hunting Stag Management Ltd. were sold to James Fisher and Sons, Barrow in July, Stag Line, Ltd. remained a subsidiary of Hunting Gibson but in November 1982 the ZINNIA was sold to Singapore buyers, then in March 1983 the BEGONIA, the remaining Stag Line ship, was also sold to Singapore buyers.

The sale of the BEGONIA highlights the end of an era, not only for Stag Line (1817-1983) but, maybe, also for British Tramp Shipping.

Stag Line records are being placed with the Tyne and Wear Archives branch office at the Local Studies Centre, Howard Street, North Shields under reference 628/- Amongst the records are:-

Ships' voyages and Crew lists from 1885, Profit and Loss accounts and Balance sheets from 1895, photocopies of Classification, Building and Survey Reports on the STAG (1846) and ROBINSONS (1856), several Hull and Machinery Specifications from 1896 (GLOXINIA I) and several Capacity Plans from 1920 (GLOXINIA II).

A detailed history of the Robinson family, and the Company, is in course of preparation and will be published shortly.

FLEET LIST NOTES

The notation '1', '2', etc., in brackets after a ship's name indicates that she is the first, second, etc., ship of that name in the fleet. The dates following the name are those of entering and leaving the fleet, or coming under and leaving the management of the Company.

On the first line is given the ship's Official Number (O.N.) in the British Registry, followed by her tonnages gross ('g') and net ('n'). Dimensions given are registered length × beam × depth in feet and tenths for ships numbered 1-68 and M.1-M.9 and the overall length × beam × draught at summer deadweight for the ships numbered 69-77.

On the second line is given the type of engines and the name of the engine builders 'C.2-cyl.' denotes compound two cylinder steam engines, 'T.3-cyl,' = triple expansion three cylinder steam engines, 'Q.4-cyl.' = quadruple expansion four cylinder steam engines and for motor vessels the number of cylinders is given and whether they are two stroke cycle (2 S.C.) or four stroke cycle (4 S.C.) single acting (S.A.).

The ships' histories are corrected up to December 1983.

FLEET LIST

1. BLESSING (1817 — 1846) Snow.
221n, 88.0 × 24.5 × 14.1 feet.
1805: Built by Benjamin Howard, Southwick, Sunderland for Nicholas and John Richardson.
7.1817: Purchased by James Robinson, Master Mariner (Sixty four shares). *5.1828:* James Robinson transferred by indenture sixty four shares to George Stroman, Shadwell who on *24.4.1832* transferred them by indenture to Robert and Richard Brown of St. Mary at Hill, London. *10.2.1833:* Captain James Robinson died and management of the vessel was transferred to his widow, Grace Robinson. *8.6.1843:* Robert and Richard Brown sold all sixty four shares to Grace and Joseph Robinson (widow and son of Captain James Robinson). *7.10.1844:* Grace Robinson died and ownership of the vessel was transferred to Joseph Robinson. *28.3.1846:* Lost off Flamborough Head.

2. STAG (1) (1846 — 1858) Snow later Brig.
ON. 130/1846. 182n, 82.5 × 21.2 × 12.9 feet.
1846: Built by Luke, Blumer and Bushell, South Shields for Joseph Robinson (28 shares), Thomas Robinson (22 shares) and James Miller (14 shares). Joseph Robinson who was Master from 23rd May 1846 to 11th October 1848 and again between 5th March 1851 and 29th June 1851 is described as a Master Mariner, Thomas Robinson as a Tailor and James Miller as a Shipowner. *26.5.1846:* Sailed on her maiden voyage from Newcastle to London with Captain Joseph Robinson in command. *12.1.1850:* Re-registered as a brig. *6.3.1858:* Sank after being run down off Southwold by an unknown vessel whilst on a voyage from Shields to London with a cargo of coal. The crew were landed safely.

3. FELLOWSHIP (1848 — 1849) Ship.
ON. 2851 (issued in 1855). 201n, 92.0 × 21.7 × 12.8 feet.
1840: Built by Nicholas Mosher, Newport, Nova Scotia as FELLOWSHIP for his own account.
1848: Sold to E. H. Hogg and *18.9.1848* re-registered at North Shields. *18.12.1848:* Purchased by Joseph Robinson, Thomas Robinson and Eleanor Johnson. *20.1.1849:* Sold to Thomas Rutherford and William Nicholson, Seaham. *1851:* Transferred to Thomas Rutherford. *1.1863:* Foundered in heavy weather 30 miles off Lowestoft whilst on a voyage from Seaham Harbour to London with a cargo of coal. All the crew were saved.

4. ELEANOR GRACE (1) (1849 — 1857) Ship.
ON. 14649. 224n, 86.8 × 22.3 × 14.6 feet.
11.1849: Completed by Thomas Seymour, Walker on Tyne for Joseph Robinson (40 shares), Thomas Robinson (16 shares) and Eleanor Johnson (8 shares). *24.2.1857:* Wrecked whilst on a voyage from Belfast to Newcastle.

5. ALBERT (1853 — 1871) Brig.
ON. 34801. 161n, 72.8 × 20.8 × 14.0 feet.
5.1842: Completed by Peter and James Tait, Stromness as ALBERT for James Spence of Stromness, a Shipmaster (8 shares) and others including George Hobbs (9 shares) and Peter Tait (5 shares). *3.10.1850:* Sold to James Leask, Kirkwall, a Master Mariner (64 shares). *19.8.1852:* Sold to Anthony Wood and Co., Newcastle upon Tyne. *30.5.1853:* Purchased by Joseph Robinson (40 shares) and Thomas Robinson (24 shares). *10.4.1856:* Registered tonnage increased to 198.69 tons. *1871:* Sold to Edward Wilkinson, Blyth. *1878:* Sold to George Smee, Maldon. *7.1.1890:* Sold to James Watson, Newcastle upon Tyne and re-registered with dimensions 92.3 × 24.2 × 13.2 feet and registered tonnage 191.29 tons. *23.5.1891:* Foundered off Sunderland.

6. ROBINSONS (1856 — 1871) Barque.
ON. 17045. 327n, 110.0 × 26.8 × 16.5 feet.
1856: Built by W. Stothard, Sunderland for Joseph Robinson (40 shares), Thomas Robinson (16 shares) and Eleanor Johnson (8 shares). *4.5.1871:* Sold to William Robinson and others, Blyth. *4.1881:* Sold to W. Svendsen, Norway and renamed ALETTE. *31.1.1886:* Wrecked on a voyage from London to Kristiansand.

7. CAMELLIA (1) (1858 — 1877) Barque.
ON. 20439. 312n, 108.4 × 26.2 × 16.8 feet.
1858: Completed at Sunderland for Joseph Robinson (44 shares) and Thomas Robinson (20 shares). *16.2.1858:* Sailed on her maiden voyage to the Mediterranean. *1869:* Lengthened by 14.6 feet to 123.0 feet and registered tonnage increased to 332 tons. *1872:* Insured value £3,300. *25.3.1877:* Wrecked at Pipas near Montevideo whilst on a voyage from Trey Ventos to the U.K. with a cargo of hides. Insured value £3,000.

8. CLINTONIA (1) (1861 — 1865) Barque.
ON. 29704. 336n, 110.0 × 26.2 × 16.7 feet.
1861: Built at Sunderland for Joseph Robinson (64 shares). *10.8.1865:* Sailed from Taganrog on a voyage to America and after sailing from Constantinople on *6.9.1865* disappeared with all hands.

9. GLADIOLUS (1) (1863 — 1879) Barque.
ON. 45601. 345g, 306n, 113.1 × 27.2 × 16.8 feet.
3.1863: Completed by John Robinson, Sunderland for Joseph Robinson and *6.4.1863* sailed on her maiden voyage to the Black Sea. *20.2.1872:* Insured value £2,800. *13.10.1879:* Wrecked at Yallachs Bay, Jamaica whilst awaiting cargo for Liverpool. Insured value £1,500.

10. STAG (2) (1866 — 1873) Barque.
ON. 53482. 296n, 111.6 × 26.0 × 16.0 feet.
8.1866: Completed by John Robinson, Sunderland for Joseph Robinson and *31.8.1866* sailed on her maiden voyage to Cronstadt. *20.2.1872:* Insured value £2,800. *30.3.1873:* Wrecked on English Bank, River Plate. Insured for £2,800 at the time of her loss.

ELEANOR GRACE   *Author's Collection*

11. ELEANOR GRACE (2) (1867 — 1879) Barque.
ON. 56499. 336n, 120.3 × 26.8 × 16.7 feet.
5.1867: Completed by John Robinson, Sunderland for Joseph Robinson and *8.6.1867* sailed on her maiden voyage to the Black Sea. *20.2.1872:* Insured value £3,200. *7.1877:* Her master, Captain John Spence, was empowered to sell the ship within nine months for not less than £3,000 but in fact no sale took place. *2.1.1879:* Sailed from Plymouth whilst on a voyage from Taganrog to Stockton on Tees with a cargo of linseed and disappeared with all hands. Insured for £2,400 at the time of her loss.

12. JOHN BARING (1870 — 1875) Barque.
ON. 30106. 547g, 124.4 × 30.2 × 23.2 feet.
1834: Built at Stonington, U.S.A. for unknown owners. *1856:* Sold to Octavius Swan and Thomas Swan (52 shares) and John Crutwell (12 shares), rigged as a ship and registered in Malta. *26.7.1859:* John Swan acquired the 52 shares from Octavius and Thomas Swan. Subsequently the ship's figurehead was changed from a man's bust to a stag's head but there is no indication of any Robinson interest in the ship at this time. *1865:* Sold to George Hurford (31 shares) and others. Re-registered as a barque. *4.1865:* Sold to Thomas Gibson (52 shares) and on his death *3.8.1865* George Hurford was appointed executor. *9.5.1870:* Joseph Robinson, the Younger, purchased 52 shares and two days later he acquired the remaining 12 shares. He then sold to Thomas Robinson (8 shares), John Robinson (8 shares), Nicholas J. Robinson (8 shares), James Hunter (8 shares) and in the following year to Joseph Green (8 shares) and William Russell (8 shares). *20.2.1872:* Insured value £1,600. *31.5.1875:* Wrecked at the mouth of the Frontenac River, Tabasco Province, Mexico whilst outward bound, under pilot's orders, with a cargo of 600 tons of mahogany and cedarwood. She was on a voyage from Belize to Tabasco and was insured for £1,600 at the time of her loss.

16

13. CADUCEUS (1870 — 1872) Barque.
ON. 12598. 411g, 395n, 660d, 124.1 × 27.8 × 18.1 feet.
3.1857: Completed by John Davison, Sunderland as CADUCEUS for Edmund H. Hogg (36 shares), John Lucas (6 shares) and others. *11.1858:* Following certain mortgage transactions, Mrs. Mary Fawcett became the principal shareholder with 28 shares. *23.3.1868:* Mrs. Mary Fawcett died and William H. Cave and Mrs. Ann Hogg (widow of Edmund H. Hogg) were appointed executors. Mrs. Ann Hogg became the principal shareholder with 28 shares together with William H. Cave (16 shares) and Mrs. D. Lucas (14 shares). *7.7.1870:* Joseph Robinson, the Younger, purchased 58 shares. *1872:* Sold to Mrs. A. Hogg and Mrs. D. Lucas. *4.1873:* Sold to Thomas Knox, North Shields. *6.1875:* Sold to James Bolt (24 shares) and others. *7.1877:* James Bolt acquired a further 8 shares. *28.11.1881:* Stranded and broke in two on Chichester Bank, near Portsmouth, whilst on a voyage from the River Tyne to Salerno with a cargo of coal.

14. TELEGRAM (1871 — 1873) Barque.
ON. 27240. 517g, 134.0 × 30.8 × 18.8 feet.
1851: Built at Somerset, Massachusetts as GREENFIELD for unknown owners and later renamed TELEGRAM. *21.5.1859:* Sold to George Croshaw, London. *3.6.1859:* Sold to John Lash, Croydon Common. *15.8.1863:* Sold to James Turpie, North Shields. *7.12.1870:* Sold to John F. Middleton (32 shares) and others, North Shields. *28.2.1871:* Purchased by Joseph Robinson, the Younger (56 shares). *3.1871:* Joseph Robinson, the Younger sold 48 shares. *20.2.1872:* Insured value £1,400. *3.2.1873:* Abandoned in the Bay of Biscay whilst on a voyage from Newport to Jamaica with a cargo of coal. At the time of her loss six shareholders held 8 shares each and one (John Hedley) held 16 shares. The vessel was insured for £1,400.

STEPHANOTIS   *York Collection*

15. STEPHANOTIS (1) (1871 — 1898) Iron Steamship.
ON. 65382. 1042g, 678n, 1530d, 220.5 × 30.6 × 19.2 feet.
2 cylinder inverted single expansion steam engine by North Eastern Marine Engineering Co., Sunderland. Replaced in 1877 by a C.2-cyl. by R. and W. Hawthorn and Co., Newcastle upon Tyne.
2.1871: Launched and *3.1871:* Completed by Iliff. Mounsey and Co., Sunderland for Joseph Robinson. Cost £16,800. *5.1871:* Joseph Robinson sold 46 shares to 17 shareholders, including Joseph Robinson, the Younger (4 shares), Nicholas J. Robinson (1 share) and Thomas Robinson (5 shares). *20.2.1872:* Insured value £18,000. *1883:* Insured value £15,000. *2.9.1895:* Transferred to "Stag Line", Ltd. for £4,608. *7.9.1898:* Sold to Robson, Brown and Sons Ltd., Sunderland. *30.4.1901:* Sank off Whitby following a collision with the British steamer GUYERS, 522/73 whilst on a voyage from Bilbao to Middlesbrough with a cargo of iron ore. The GUYERS was also lost.

16. WELLINGTON (1871) Barque.
527g, 487n, 122.4 × 29.9 × 20.0 feet.
1847: Built at Sunderland for Mr. Fenwick. *19.10.1871:* Purchased by Joseph Robinson, the Younger. *16.12.1871:* Foundered off Madeira after being abandoned in heavy weather whilst on a voyage from the River Tyne to Guadeloupe with a cargo of coal.

17. NYMPHAEA (1) (1871 — 1881) Iron Steamship.
ON. 65410. 1138g, 739n, 230.6 × 30.1 × 18.0 feet.
C.2-cyl. by North Eastern Marine Engineering Co., Sunderland.
2.9.1871: Launched by Iliff, Mounsey and Co., Sunderland for Joseph Robinson. Cost £15,940. *20.2.1872:* Insured value £18,000. *28.10.1872:* Joseph Robinson sold 45 shares to 18 shareholders, including Nicholas J. Robinson (4 shares) and Joseph Robinson, the Younger (4 shares). *1880:* Insured value £16,000. *4.1.1881:* Wrecked on Sunk Sand at the entrance to the River Thames whilst on a voyage from Shields to Piraeus with a cargo of coal.

18. NUPHAR (1) (1872 — 1878) Iron Steamship.
ON. 65445. 1137g, 731n, 230.5 × 30.0 × 18.2 feet.
C.2-cyl. by North Eastern Marine Engineering Co., Sunderland.
8.1872: Launched by Iliff, Mounsey and Co., Sunderland for Joseph Robinson. *21.10.1873:* Joseph Robinson sold 47 shares to 21 shareholders, including Nicholas J. Robinson (4 shares) and Joseph Robinson, the Younger (4 shares). *12.12.1878:* Stranded and broke in two near Honfleur whilst on a voyage from Konigsberg to Rouen with a cargo of wheat and flax. Insured for £17,000 at the time of her loss.

19. DANAE (1873 — 1877). Iron Steamship.
ON. 65456. 1157g, 745n, 230.0 × 30.3 × 18.2 feet.
C.2-cyl. by North Eastern Marine Engineering Co., Sunderland.
1.1873: Launched by Iliff, Mounsey and Co., Sunderland for Joseph Robinson and on delivery insured for £21,000. *3.3.1874:* Joseph Robinson sold 48 shares to 23 shareholders, including Nicholas J. Robinson (2 shares) and Joseph Robinson, the Younger (4 shares). *25.12.1877:* Foundered off Horns Reef whilst on a voyage from Copenhagen and Reval to London with a cargo of wheat. Insured for £17,000 at the time of her loss.

20. STAG (3) (1874 — 1880) Iron Steamship.
ON. 70386. 1558g, 1006n, 259.4 × 33.5 × 24.3 feet.
C.2-cyl. by North Eastern Marine Engineering Co., Sunderland.
8.1874: Launched by Bartram, Haswell and Co., Sunderland for Joseph Robinson and Co. Cost £30,300 and on delivery insured for £32,000. *2.10.1880:* Wrecked at Punta Delgada, Azores after colliding with the company's steamer ROBINIA 1816/76 when her anchors dragged during a fierce gale. She was on a voyage from New Orleans to Marseilles. Insured for £28,000 at the time of her loss.

21. AMY DORA (1875 — 1889) Iron Steamship.
ON. 70402. 1708g, 1107n, 265.0 × 34.0 × 24.4 feet.
C. 2-cyl. by North Eastern Marine Engineering Co., Sunderland.
6.1875: Launched by Cole Bros., Newcastle upon Tyne for Joseph Robinson and Co. Cost £28,800 and on delivery insured for £30,000. *1883:* Insured value reduced to £27,000. *5.10.1889:* Wrecked on Watchapreague Shoals, Virginia whilst on a voyage from Savannah via Newport News to Genoa with a cargo of cotton.

22. AMARYLLIS (1) (1875 — 1899) Iron Steamship.
ON. 70405. 1714g, 1109n, 2575d, 264.4 × 34.0 × 24.3 feet.
C. 2-cyl. by North Eastern Marine Engineering Co., Sunderland.
10.1875: Launched by Cole Bros., Newcastle upon Tyne for Joseph Robinson and Co. Cost £28,000 and on delivery insured for £30,000. *1883:* Insured value reduced to £27,000. *30.9.1895:* Transferred to "Stag Line", Ltd. for £6,912. *1899:* Sold to Amaryllis Shipping Co. Ltd. (W. Coupland and Co. managers), Newcastle upon Tyne. *7.11.1900:* Foundered off Ushant after a collision with the German steamer INDIA, 1551/81 whilst on a voyage from the River Tyne to Savona with a cargo of coal. When the collision occurred, the INDIA was attempting to take the crew off the AMARYLLIS, which was drifting without power and listing heavily.

23. CYDONIA (1) (1876 — 1899) Iron Steamship.
ON. 70415. 1693g, 1093n, 2540d, 265.0 × 34.0 × 24.4 feet.
C. 2-cyl. by North Eastern Marine Engineering Co., Sunderland.
4.1876: Launched by Cole Bros., Newcastle upon Tyne for Joseph Robinson and Co. Cost £28,220 and on delivery insured for £30,000. *19.10.1895:* Transferred to "Stag Line", Ltd. for £6,912. *1899:* Sold to Dunford and Elliott, Newcastle upon Tyne. *1904:* Sold to Doi Kametaro, Japan and renamed NANIWA MARU. *1910:* Sold to K. Yokoyama, Japan. *1912:* Sold to C. Tanaka, Japan. *1920:* Sold to Tanaka Kozan Kabushiki Kaisha, Japan. *8.7.1922:* Wrecked at Shikotsisaki whilst on a voyage from Muroran to Kamaishi with a cargo of coal and beans. She later slipped off the rocks and sank in deep water.

CYDONIA *Author's Collection*

24. ROBINIA (1) (1876 — 1880) Iron Steamship.
ON. 76631. 1816g, 1181n, 280.5 × 34.0 × 24.6 feet.
C. 2-cyl. by North Eastern Marine Engineering Co., Sunderland.
12.1876: Launched by C. Mitchell and Co., Newcastle upon Tyne for Joseph Robinson and Co. Cost £28,500 and on delivery insured for £31,000. *2.10.1880:* Wrecked at Punta Delgada, Azores after colliding with the company's steamer STAG 1558/74 and the British steamer BENELLA 1229/80 when all three vessels dragged their anchors during a fierce gale. She was on a voyage from New Orleans to Le Havre. Insured for £29,000 at the time of her loss.

25. AZALEA (1877 — 1897) Iron Steamship.
ON. 76634. 1828g, 1188n, 2637d, 280.5 × 34.0 × 24.6 feet.
C. 2-cyl. by North Eastern Marine Engineering Co., Sunderland.
2.1877: Launched by C. Mitchell and Co., Newcastle upon Tyne for Joseph Robinson and Co. Cost £28,850 and on delivery insured for £31,000. *1883:* Insured value reduced to £28,000. *26.9.1895:* Transferred to "Stag Line", Ltd. for £7,488. *21.11.1897:* Sailed from Baltimore bound for Stettin and, after passing Cape Henry the following day, disappeared with all hands.

AZALEA *York Collection*

19

26. LAURESTINA (1) (1877 — 1878) Iron Steamship.
ON. 76650. 1919g, 1238n, 286.2 × 34.2 × 24.8 feet.
C. 2-cyl. by North Eastern Marine Engineering Co., Sunderland.
9.1877: Launched by Tyne Iron Shipbuilding Co., Newcastle upon Tyne for Joseph Robinson and
Co. *29.12.1878:* Wrecked at Kopparsten Rocks, Sandhamn whilst on a voyage from Reval to
Rotterdam with a cargo of grain.

27. CAMELLIA (2) (1878 — 1898) Iron Steamship.
ON. 79208. 1363g, 880n, 1975d, 258.0 × 32.0 × 21.2 feet.
C. 2-cyl. by North Eastern Marine Engineering Co., Sunderland.
8.1878: Launched by Tyne Iron Shipbuilding Co., Newcastle upon Tyne for Joseph Robinson and
Co. Cost £20,780 and on delivery insured for £23,000. *1883:* Insured value reduced to
£21,000. *2.9.1895:* Transferred to "Stag Line", Ltd for £6,912. *1898:* Sold to Tyneside Line Ltd.
(J. Ridley, Son and Tully managers), Newcastle upon Tyne. *16.5.1910:* Extensively damaged in
a collision off Cross Sands with the British steamer WINKFIELD, 4009/00 whilst on a voyage
from Ghent to the River Tyne in ballast. Arrived in the Tyne and found to be not worth repairing.
Sold to R. Blake and broken up at Sunderland.

28. EGLANTINE (1878 — 1898) Iron Steamship.
ON. 79212. 1357g, 874n, 1975d, 258.0 × 32.0 × 21.1 feet.
C. 2-cyl. by North Eastern Marine Engineering Co., Sunderland.
9.1878: Launched by Tyne Iron Shipbuilding Co., Newcastle upon Tyne for Joseph Robinson and
Co. Cost £20,780 and on delivery insured for £23,000. *1883:* Insured value reduced to
£21,000. *27.9.1895:* Transferred to "Stag Line", Ltd. for £6,912. *1898:* Sold to Tyneside Line
Ltd. (J. Ridley, Son and Tully managers), Newcastle upon Tyne. *16.4.1915:* Wrecked on Filey
Brig during an attempt to avoid an enemy submarine whilst on a voyage from the River Tyne to
Le Havre with a cargo of coal.

29. CORONILLA (1878 — 1898) Iron Steamship.
ON. 79215. 1361g, 875n, 1975d, 258.0 × 32.0 × 21.1 feet.
C. 2-cyl. by North Eastern Marine Engineering Co., Sunderland. Replaced in 1906 by a T. 3-cyl.
by North Eastern Marine Engineering Co. Ltd., Newcastle upon Tyne.
12.1878: Launched by Tyne Iron Shipbuilding Co., Newcastle upon Tyne for Joseph Robinson
and Co. Cost £20,780 and on delivery insured for £23,000. *1883:* Insured value reduced to
£21,000. *16.9.1895:* Transferred to "Stag Line", Ltd. for £6,912. *1898:* Sold to Tyneside Line
Ltd. (J. Ridley, Son and Tully managers), Newcastle upon Tyne. *8.1919:* Sold to Llewellyn
Shipping Co., Cardiff. *11.1919:* Sold to J. G. Bouboulis, Greece and renamed BOUBOULINA.
8.6.1921: Mined and sunk off Englezonissia, Gulf of Smyrna, whilst on a voyage from Smyrna
to Piraeus.

GARDENIA   *Author's Collection*

20

30. GARDENIA (1) (1879 — 1901) Iron Steamship.
ON. 79224. 1967g, 1276n, 2700d, 280.0 × 35.0 × 24.7 feet.
C. 2-cyl. by North Eastern Marine Engineering Co., Sunderland.
8.1879: Launched by Tyne Iron Shipbuilding Co., Newcastle upon Tyne for Joseph Robinson and Co. Cost £28,000 and on delivery insured for £30,000. *1883:* Insured value reduced to £29,000. *2.10.1895:* Transferred to "Stag Line", Ltd for £9,216. *1901:* Sold to Montauk Steam Ship Co. Ltd. (W. Coupland and Co. managers), Newcastle upon Tyne. *4.10.1913:* Sank with the loss of 18 crew following a collision with the British steamer CORNWOOD, 2152/11 near Middle Cross Sand, North Sea. She had been on a voyage from Benisaf to Middlesbrough with a cargo of iron ore.

31. VIOLA (1879 — 1900) Iron Steamship.
ON. 79226. 1963g, 1270n, 280.0 × 35.0 × 24.7 feet.
C. 2-cyl. by North Eastern Marine Engineering Co., Sunderland.
10.1879: Launched by Tyne Iron Shipbuilding Co., Newcastle upon Tyne for Joseph Robinson and Co. Cost £28,000 and on delivery insured for £30,000. *1883:* Insured value reduced to £29,000. *4.9.1895:* Transferred to "Stag Line", Ltd. for £9,216. *1900:* Sold to Montauk Steam Ship Co. Ltd. (W. Coupland and Co. managers), Newcastle upon Tyne. *19.9.1903:* Wrecked in thick fog ½ mile S. of Kettleness Point, near Whitby, whilst on a voyage from Carthagena to Middlesbrough with a cargo of iron ore. Her crew of 20 men was rescued by the Runswick lifeboat and two weeks later the vessel broke in half.

32. GLADIOLUS (2) (1880 — 1901) Iron Steamship.
ON. 79237. 1941g, 1258n, 2729d, 280.6 × 36.0 × 22.6 feet.
C. 2-cyl. by North Eastern Marine Engineering Co., Sunderland.
7.1880: Launched by Tyne Iron Shipbuilding Co., Newcastle upon Tyne for Joseph Robinson and Co. Cost £26,500 and on delivery insured for £28,000. *1883:* Insured value increased to £29,000. *18.9.1895:* Transferred to "Stag Line", Ltd. for £10,368. *1901:* Sold to Amaryllis Shipping Co. Ltd. (W. Coupland and Co. managers), Newcastle upon Tyne. *1912:* Sold to C.H.C. Sunderman and broken up at Dordrecht.

33. CLINTONIA (2) (1881 — 1897) Iron Steamship.
ON. 84857. 1970g, 1287n, 2850d, 287.0 × 37.0 × 21.8 feet.
C. 2-cyl. by North Eastern Marine Engineering Co., Sunderland.
8.1881: Launched by Tyne Iron Shipbuilding Co., Newcastle upon Tyne for Joseph Robinson and Co. Cost £27,900 and on delivery insured for £30,000. *24.10.1895:* Transferred to "Stag Line", Ltd. for £10,944. *26.4.1897:* Severely damaged by fire at Newport News after arriving from Cuba and declared a constructive total loss. Sold to L. Luckenbach, U.S.A. and converted to a barge. *1903:* Transferred to Luckenbach Transportation and Wrecking Co., U.S.A. *1909:* Transferred to Estate, of L. Luckenbach, U.S.A. *1911:* Transferred to E. F. Luckenbach, U.S.A. *4.4.1915:* Abandoned in a position 35.12N. 74.51W. whilst on a voyage from Brunswick to Newhaven, Conn. with a cargo of railroad ties.

34. IXIA (1) (1881 — 1916) Iron Steamship.
ON. 84858. 1970g, 1254n, 2850d 287.0 × 37.0 × 21.9 feet.
C. 2-cyl. by North Eastern Marine Engineering Co., Sunderland.
10.1881: Launched by Tyne Iron Shipbuilding Co., Newcastle upon Tyne for Joseph Robinson and Co. Cost £27,900 and on delivery insured for £30,000. *14.10.1895:* Transferred to "Stag Line", Ltd. for £10,944. *1911:* Fitted for the carriage of molasses in bulk. *1916:* Sold to Tres Ltd. (Houlder, Middleton and Co. Ltd. managers), London. *1917:* Renamed SAGUA. *1921:* Sold to United States Food Products Corp., U.S.A. *1922:* Sold to Sagua Corporation, (C. D. Mallory and Co. managers), Dominica. *1923:* Sold to Macoris S.S. Corporation, Dominica. *1930:* Sold to shipbreakers.

35. NUPHAR (2) (1881 — 1882) Iron Steamship.
ON. 84860. 1963g, 1280n, 2850d, 287.0 × 37.0 × 21.9 feet.
C. 2-cyl. by North Eastern Marine Engineering Co., Sunderland.
11.1881: Launched by Tyne Iron Shipbuilding Co. Newcastle upon Tyne for Joseph Robinson and Co. Insured on delivery for £30,000. *23.9.1882:* Wrecked at Cape May whilst on a voyage from Shields to Philadelphia with a cargo of pig iron.

21

NYMPHAEA ashore N. of Aberdeen.   *Author's Collection*

36. NYMPHAEA (2) (1882 — 1914) Iron Steamship.
ON. 84861. 1969g, 1249n, 2874d, 286.9 × 37.0 × 21.8 feet.
C. 2-cyl. by North Eastern Marine Engineering Co., Sunderland.
1.1882: Launched by Tyne Iron Shipbuilding Co., Newcastle upon Tyne for Joseph Robinson and Co. Cost £28,900 and on delivery insured for £30,000. *11.12.1895:* Transferred to "Stag Line", Ltd. for £10,944. *1908:* Fitted for the carriage of molasses in bulk. *14.7.1914:* Wrecked 25 miles N. of Aberdeen whilst on a voyage from the River Tyne to Cienfuegos, Cuba in ballast.

37. STAG (4) (1884 — 1916) Iron Steamship.
ON. 84899. 2052g, 1302n, 2890d, 287.0 × 37.0 × 22.0 feet.
C. 2-cyl. by North Eastern Marine Engineering Co. Ltd., Newcastle upon Tyne.
3.1884: Launched by Tyne Iron Shipbuilding Co. Ltd., Newcastle upon Tyne for Joseph Robinson and Sons. Cost £31,250. *2.10.1895:* Transferred to "Stag Line", Ltd. for £13,248. *1907:* Fitted for the carriage of molasses in bulk. *1916:* Sold to Tres Ltd. (Houlder, Middleton and Co. Ltd. managers), London. *1917:* Renamed MACORIS. *1921:* Sold to Macoris S.S. Corporation, Dominica. *1923:* Sold to Luigi Ghio, Italy to be broken up at Venice. *4.1.1924:* Foundered off Crete whilst on her final voyage from Piraeus to Venice in ballast.

38. LAURESTINA (2) (1884 — 1895) Iron Steamship.
ON. 89794. 2051g, 1336n, 2900d, 287.0 × 37.0 × 22.0 feet.
C. 2-cyl. by North Eastern Marine Engineering Co. Ltd., Newcastle upon Tyne.
5.1884: Launched by Tyne Iron Shipbuilding Co. Ltd., Newcastle upon Tyne for Joseph Robinson and Sons. Cost £31,250. *5.10.1895:* Transferred to "Stag Line", Ltd. for £13,248. *6.12.1895:* Sailed from Baltimore bound for Sligo and, after passing Cape Henry on the following day, disappeared with her crew of 25 men.

NYMPHAEA ashore, note the deck arrangement
for the carriage of molasses in bulk. *Author's Collection.*

39. ROBINIA (2) (1884 — 1904) Iron Steamship.
ON. 89798. 2058g, 1314n, 2900d, 287.0 × 37.0 × 22.1 feet.
C. 2-cyl. by North Eastern Marine Engineering Co. Ltd., Newcastle upon Tyne.
8.1884: Launched by Tyne Iron Shipbuilding Co. Ltd., Newcastle upon Tyne for Joseph Robinson
and Sons. Cost £31,250. *30.9.1895:* Transferred to "Stag Line", Ltd. for £13,248. *1904:* Sold
to D. Bozzo fu Nicolo, Italy for £5,950. *1905:* Renamed CONCETTA B. *1910:* Sold to D. & E. Flli
Bozzo, Italy. *1915:* Sold to Ditta Giovanni Pantaleo, Italy and renamed G. PANTALEO. *1916:*
Sold to Liguria Commerciale di Nav., Italy and renamed ALBERTO. *6.10.1916:* Mined and sunk
12 miles from Cape Carovedo.

ROBINIA *Author's Collection*

23

GLOXINIA as CANDINA   *World Ship Photo Library*

40. GLOXINIA (1) (1897 — 1916) Steel Steamship.
ON. 105217. 2540g, 1618n, 4310d, 313.0 × 45.0 × 20.7 feet.
T. 3-cyl. by North Eastern Marine Engineering Co. Ltd., Newcastle upon Tyne.
1.1897: Completed by Tyne Iron Shipbuilding Co. Ltd., Newcastle upon Tyne for "Stag Line",
Ltd. Cost £27,860. *1.1916:* Sold to Bolivian General Enterprise Ltd. (Leopold Walford (London)
Ltd. managers), London and renamed PETINGAUDET. *1921:* Sold to M. V. Uravain, Spain and
renamed FRANCISCA URAVAIN. *1928:* Sold to Velilla y Candina Soc. Ltda., Spain and renamed
CANDINA. *1930:* Sold to Cia. Nav. Bidasoa (A. Candina and Co. managers), Spain *1941:* Sold
to Cia. Nav. Espanola S.A., Spain. *1966:* Sold to Spanish shipbreakers and arrived at Santander
on *8.6.1966* to be broken up.

CLEMATIS   *Author's Collection*

41. CLEMATIS (1898 — 1916) Steel Steamship.
ON. 109887. 3406g, 2161n, 5717d, 344.5 × 46.0 × 16.8 feet.
T. 3-cyl. by North Eastern Marine Engineering Co. Ltd., Newcastle upon Tyne.
7.1898: Completed by Tyne Iron Shipbuilding Co. Ltd., Newcastle upon Tyne for "Stag Line",
Ltd. Cost £33,800. *1916:* Sold to Leeston Shipping Co. Ltd., Cardiff. *1920:* Sold to John Holt
and Co. (Liverpool) Ltd., Liverpool. *1926:* Sold to Societa Anon. Marittima Catanese (G. Napoli
and Figli managers), Italy. *1929:* Sold to Italian shipbreakers.

BEGONIA   *Author's Collection*

42. BEGONIA (1) (1899 — 1916) Steel Steamship.
ON. 109908. 3653g, 2346n, 5712d, 344.9 × 46.0 × 16.9 feet.
T. 3-cyl. by North Eastern Marine Engineering Co. Ltd., Newcastle upon Tyne.
12.1899: Completed by Tyne Iron Shipbuilding Co. Ltd., Newcastle upon Tyne for "Stag Line",
Ltd. Cost £38,750. *1916:* Sold to Maindy Shipping Co. Ltd. (Jenkins, Richards and Evans Ltd.
managers), Cardiff and renamed MAINDY BRIDGE. *8.12.1917:* Torpedoed and sunk by a German
submarine 4 miles E.N.E. of Sunderland whilst on a voyage from Middlesbrough to the River
Tyne in ballast. Two members of the crew were lost.

BEGONIA at Reunion   *K. O'Donoghue Collection*

ZINNIA   *H. S. Appleyard Collection*

43. ZINNIA (1) (1900 — 1912) Steel Steamship.
ON. 113064. 3642g, 2339n, 5717d, 345.0 × 46.1 × 16.9 feet.
T. 3-cyl. by North Eastern Marine Engineering Co. Ltd., Newcastle upon Tyne.
2.1900: Completed by Tyne Iron Shipbuilding Co. Ltd., Newcastle upon Tyne for "Stag Line",
Ltd. Cost £38,750. *27.3.1912:* Beached off Cape Comorin after a fire had broken out during a
voyage from Calcutta to Karachi with a cargo of coal. Subsequently declared a total loss.

STEPHANOTIS   *Author's Collection*

26

44. STEPHANOTIS (2) (1904 — 1915) Steel Steamship.
ON. 117961. 4060g, 2584n, 6309d, 350.0 × 48.0 × 17.9 feet.
T. 3-cyl. by North Eastern Marine Engineering Co. Ltd., Newcastle upon Tyne.
5.1904: Completed by Tyne Iron Shipbuilding Co. Ltd., Newcastle upon Tyne for "Stag Line",
Ltd. Cost £38,750. *17.6.1915:* Sold to Hackensack S.S. Co. Ltd. (Brown, Jenkinson and Co.
managers), London and renamed HACKENSACK. *25.4.1917:* Torpedoed and sunk 180 miles
N.W. by W. of Fastnet by the German submarine U.82 whilst on a voyage from Cienfuegos and
Halifax to Queenstown with a cargo of sugar. Six of her crew were lost.

AMARYLLIS at Torrevieja in March 1906   *Author's Collection*

45. AMARYLLIS (2) (1904 — 1908) Steel Steamship.
ON. 117962. 4064g, 2587n, 6309d, 350.0 × 48.0 × 17.9 feet.
T. 3-cyl. by North Eastern Marine Engineering Co. Ltd., Newcastle upon Tyne.
7.1904: Completed by Tyne Iron Shipbuilding Co. Ltd., Newcastle upon Tyne for "Stag Line",
Ltd. Cost £38,750. *7.2.1908:* Wrecked at Kalkudah, Ceylon whilst on a voyage from Calcutta
to Bombay with a cargo of coal. £34,601 paid by insurers.

46. EUPHORBIA (1) (1907 — 1916) Steel Steamship.
ON. 117972. 3837g, 2444n, 6600d, 350.1 × 50.1 × 22.4 feet.
T. 3-cyl. by the Shipbuilders.
1907: Completed by W. Doxford and Sons Ltd., Sunderland for "Stag Line", Ltd. Cost £38,901.
16.7.1916: Torpedoed and sunk 56 miles N.E. of Algiers by the German submarine U.39 whilst
on a voyage from Calcutta to London with general cargo. Eleven of her crew were lost.

47. CLINTONIA (3) (1907 — 1915) Steel Steamship.
ON. 117975. 3830g, 2440n, 6600d, 350.1 × 50.1 × 22.4 feet.
T. 3-cyl. by the Shipbuilders.
1907: Completed by W. Doxford and Sons Ltd., Sunderland for "Stag Line", Ltd. Cost £38,901.
1.8.1915: Torpedoed and sunk 30 miles S.W. by W. of Ushant by the German submarine U.28
whilst on a voyage from Marseilles to the River Tyne in ballast. Ten members of her crew were
lost.

CYDONIA at Manchester   *Author's Collection*

48. CYDONIA (2) (1910 — 1916) Steel Steamship.
ON. 127107. 3085g, 1890n, 5370d, 331.5 × 48.0 × 22.2 feet.
T. 3-cyl. by North Eastern Marine Engineering Co. Ltd., Newcastle upon Tyne.
1910: Completed by W. Dobson and Co., Newcastle upon Tyne for "Stag Line", Ltd. Cost £30,226. *1914:* Requisitioned by the Admiralty. *27.9.1916:* Wrecked on Castle Rocks, Holy Island whilst on a voyage from Burntisland to Brest with a cargo of coal.

LINARIA   *G. Scott Collection*

49. LINARIA (1) (1911 — 1914) Steel Steamship.
ON. 127121. 3081g, 1881n, 5340d, 331.4 × 48.0 × 22.2 feet.
T. 3-cyl. by North Eastern Marine Engineering Co. Ltd., Newcastle upon Tyne.
1911: Completed by W. Dobson and Co., Newcastle upon Tyne for "Stag Line", Ltd. Cost £32,778. *26.12.1914:* Mined and sunk $2\frac{1}{2}$ miles N.N.E. of Filey whilst on a voyage from London to the River Tyne in ballast.

PHOTINIA *Author's Collection*

50. PHOTINIA (1) (1913 — 1917) Steel Steamship.
ON. 133314. 4584g, 2835n, 8300d, 383.0 × 51.7 × 26.6 feet.
T. 3-cyl. by G. Clark Ltd., Sunderland.
7.1913: Completed by W. Pickersgill and Sons Ltd., Sunderland for "Stag Line", Ltd. Cost £57,122. *1917:* Sold to National S.S. Co. Ltd. (Fisher, Alimonda and Co. Ltd. managers), London and renamed FOTINIA. *1929:* Management transferred to J. and C. Harrison Ltd. *1932:* Sold to S. Perivolaris, Greece and renamed MARGARITIS. *1939:* Sold to Mrs. A. Perry (S. Perivolaris manager), Panama and renamed AURORA. *1941:* Sold to Kokoku Kisen K.K., Japan and renamed EIZAN MARU. *18.1.1942:* Torpedoed and sunk by the American submarine PLUNGER in a position 33.30N. 135.00E.

GARDENIA as CRANDON *E. N. Taylor*

51. GARDENIA (2) (1914 — 1923) Steel Steamship.
ON. 133327. 3108g, 1899n, 5350d, 331.2 × 48.0 × 22.2 feet.
T. 3-cyl. by North Eastern Marine Engineering Co. Ltd., Newcastle upon Tyne.
1914: Completed by Tyne Iron Shipbuilding Co. Ltd., Newcastle upon Tyne for "Stag Line", Ltd. Cost £44,337. *1923:* Sold to Charlton Steam Shipping Co. Ltd. (Charlton, McAllum and Co. Ltd. managers), Newcastle upon Tyne and renamed HAVENSIDE. *1927:* Sold to Crandon Shipping Co. Ltd., Cardiff and renamed CRANDON. *1933:* Sold to New Era S.S. Co. Ltd. (Frank S. Dawson Ltd. managers), Newcastle upon Tyne and renamed DAVID DAWSON. *1935:* Sold to Sovtorgflot, U.S.S.R. and renamed KUZBASS. *26.9.1944:* Wrecked in a position 64.25N. 173.57W. whilst on a voyage from Ugolnaya Bay to Providenia.

52. CAMELLIA (3) (1914 — 1917) Steel Steamship.
ON. 133525. 3157g, 1957n, 5500d, 331.0 × 47.7 × 22.5 feet.
T. 3-cyl. by J. Dickinson and Sons Ltd., Sunderland.
2.1913: Completed by J. Blumer and Co., Sunderland as TYNEHOME for Home Shipping Co. Ltd.
(Common Bros. managers), Newcastle upon Tyne. *29.12.1914:* Purchased by "Stag Line", Ltd.
for £42,000 and renamed CAMELLIA. *27.11.1917:* Sailed from Dakar on a voyage to the U.K.
and disappeared with all hands.

53. CLINTONIA (4) (1917 — 1940) Steel Steamship.
ON. 139879. 3106g, 1882n, 5330d, 331.0 × 48.0 × 22.2 feet.
T. 3-cyl. by North Eastern Marine Engineering Co. Ltd., Newcastle upon Tyne.
1917: Completed by W. Dobson and Co., Newcastle upon Tyne for "Stag Line", Ltd. Cost
£71,515. *19.10.1940:* Torpedoed by the German submarine U.99 and sunk by gunfire from the
German submarine U.123 W. of St. Kilda in a position 57.10N. 11.20W. The ship was sailing
in Convoy S.C.7 at the time of the sinking and was on a voyage from St. Francis N.S. to
Manchester with a cargo of pulpwood.

CLINTONIA at Hull   *Author's Collection*

54. EUPHORBIA (2) (1917) Steel Steamship.
ON. 139880. 3109g, 1887n, 5350d, 331.1 × 48.0 × 22.2 feet.
T. 3-cyl. by North Eastern Marine Engineering Co. Ltd., Newcastle upon Tyne.
1917: Completed by W. Dobson and Co., Newcastle upon Tyne for "Stag Line", Ltd. Cost
£75,508. *1.12.1917:* Torpedoed and sunk 14 miles E. by S. from the Royal Sovereign lightship
by the German submarine UC.75 whilst on a voyage from Bassein to London with a cargo of rice.
Fourteen members of the crew were lost.

55. BEGONIA (2) (1918) Steel Steamship.
ON. 139882. 2929g, 1783n, 5000d, 331.0 × 48.0 × 22.2 feet.
T. 3-cyl. by North Eastern Marine Engineering Co. Ltd., Newcastle upon Tyne.
1918: Completed by W. Dobson and Co., Newcastle upon Tyne for "Stag Line", Ltd. Cost
£94,801. *21.3.1918:* Torpedoed and sunk 44 miles S. by W. from Wolf Rock by the German
submarine UB.55 whilst on a voyage from the River Tyne and Plymouth to Salonica with
Admiralty cargo.

GLOXINIA laid up at Stanhope Buoys, R. Tyne   *J. Cleet Collection*

56. GLOXINIA (2) (1920 — 1952) Steel Steam Tanker.
ON. 139896. 3336g, 1961n, 5542d, 331.5 × 47.9 × 23.0 feet.
T. 3-cyl. by North Eastern Marine Engineering Co. Ltd., Newcastle upon Tyne.
9.1920: Completed by Tyne Iron Shipbuilding Co. Ltd., Newcastle upon Tyne for Stag Line, Ltd. as a dry cargo ship. *4.1921:* Delivered after conversion to a tanker by Smith's Dock Co. Ltd., North Shields. Cost, including conversion, £236,235. *7.1952:* Sold to Imera Siciliana di Nav., Italy for £115,000 and renamed VITTORIA O. *1955:* Sold to "SOARMA" Soc. Armamento Marittimo, Italy and converted to a dry cargo ship. *3.4.1959:* Arrived at Spezia to be broken up by Cantieri Navali Santa Maria.

GLOXINIA leaving the R. Tyne, note the modified funnel   *Author's Collection*

IXIA *York Collection*

57. IXIA (2) (1922 — 1929) Steel Steamship.
ON. 139897. 2985g, 1828n, 5010d, 331.0 × 47.7 × 21.9 feet.
T. 3-cyl. by J. Dickinson and Sons Ltd., Sunderland.
7.1922: Completed by J. Blumer and Co. Ltd., Sunderland for Stag Line, Ltd. having been originally ordered by Norwegian owners. Cost £44,706. *30.6.1929:* Wrecked on The Brisons, Cape Cornwall, whilst on a voyage from Swansea to Constantinople with a cargo of coal.

58. LINARIA (2) (1924 — 1941) Steel Steamship.
ON. 139904. 3385g, 2014n, 5700d, 331.0 × 48.0 × 23.2 feet.
T. 3-cyl. by North Eastern Marine Engineering Co. Ltd., Sunderland.
1924: Completed by Sunderland Shipbuilding Co. Ltd., Sunderland for Stag Line, Ltd. Cost £58,633. *24.2.1941:* Torpedoed and sunk by the Italian submarine BIANCHI in a position 61N. 25W. approx. whilst on a voyage from the River Tyne and Loch Ewe to Halifax N.S. The ship had been sailing in Convoy O.B. 288 which had been ordered to disperse. Her crew of 35 men was lost.

LINARIA *J. Clarkson*

EUPHORBIA   *G. Scott Collection*

59. EUPHORBIA (3) (1924 — 1940) Steel Steamship.
ON. 139905. 3380g, 2011n, 5700d, 331.0 × 48.0 × 23.2 feet.
T. 3-cyl. by North Eastern Marine Engineering Co. Ltd., Sunderland.
1924: Completed by Sunderland Shipbuilding Co. Ltd., Sunderland for Stag Line, Ltd. Cost
£57,745. *14.12.1940:* Torpedoed and sunk by the German submarine U.100 in the North
Atlantic whilst on a voyage from Swansea and Milford Haven to Lynn, Massachusetts. Her crew
of 33 men and 1 gunner were lost.

60. CYDONIA (3) (1927 — 1949) Steel Steamship.
ON. 148802. 3517g, 2175n, 6493d, 356.3 × 48.7 × 23.9 feet.
T. 3-cyl. by J. Dickinson and Sons Ltd., Sunderland.
1922: Laid down by J. Blumer and Co. Ltd., Sunderland but not launched until 3.12.1926 as the
shipyard had been closed in the meantime. *1.1927:* Completed for Stag Line, Ltd. Cost £58,000.
21.10.1949: Severely damaged by a mine 32 miles N. of Strumble Head whilst on a voyage
from Workington to Cardiff and beached on the following day. *2.11.1949:* Refloated but found
to be damaged beyond economical repair. Sold to British Iron and Steel Corporation, allocated
to T.W. Ward Ltd. and broken up at Milford Haven. Insurance paid £103,516.

CYDONIA   *Author's Collection*

GARDENIA   *York Collection*

61. GARDENIA (3) (1928 — 1940) Steel Steamship.
ON. 148804. 3745g, 2316n, 6495d, 360.8 × 48.3 × 25.1 feet.
T. 3-cyl. by the Shipbuilders.
18.4.1928: Launched by Armstrong, Whitworth and Co. Ltd., Newcastle upon Tyne as
STRONGARM, having been built as a speculation. *12.1928:* Completed as GARDENIA for Stag
Line, Ltd. *12.3.1940:* Mined and sunk N.E. of Cromer in a position 53.04N. 01.33E whilst on a
voyage from Casablanca to Billingham and Leith with a cargo of phosphates.

PHOTINIA   *Author's Collection*

62. PHOTINIA (2) (1938 — 1950) Steel Steamship.
ON. 161545. 4010g, 2457n, 6750d, 364.5 × 50.7 × 24.4 feet.
T. 3-cyl. by North Eastern Marine Engineering Co. Ltd., Sunderland.
12.1929: Completed by Swan, Hunter and Wigham Richardson Ltd., Sunderland as HOPEDENE
for Hopemount Shipping Co. Ltd. (A. Stott and Co. Ltd. managers), Newcastle upon Tyne. *1938:*
Purchased by Stag Line, Ltd. for £46,736 and renamed PHOTINIA. *1948:* Converted from coal
to oil burning. *1950:* Sold to Rederi A/B Asta (Arthur Andersson, manager), Finland for
£110,000 and renamed ATLAS. *1956:* Management transferred to Lennart Karlsson. *1968:*
Sold to Cia. de Nav. Pinares S.A., Somaliland. *1973:* Sold to Brodospas and *22.1.1974:* arrived
at Split to be broken up.

BEGONIA *Author's Collection*

63. ELIZABETH MASSEY/BEGONIA (3) (1943 — 1956) Steel Steamship.
ON. 162690. 4323g, 2598n, 7718d, 370.5 × 51.7 × 25.4 feet.
T. 3-cyl. by North Eastern Marine Engineering Co. Ltd., Sunderland.
7.1929: Completed by W. Doxford and Sons Ltd., Sunderland as JULIET for Hans Hannevig, Norway. *1931:* Sold to Essex Line Ltd. (Meldrum and Swinson, managers), London and renamed ESSEX NOBLE. *1933:* Sold to The Red "R" Steamship Co. Ltd. (Stephens, Sutton Ltd., managers), Newcastle upon Tyne and renamed REAVELEY. *1939:* Sold to W. A. Massey and Sons Ltd., Hull and renamed ELIZABETH MASSEY. *1943:* Purchased by Stag Line, Ltd. for £80,495. *1945:* Renamed BEGONIA. *1949:* Converted from coal to oil burning at a cost of £16,080. *1956:* Sold to Pio Tomei, Italy for £250,000 and renamed PEONIA. *1964:* Sold to Cantieri Navali del Golfo who commenced demolition *11.5.1964* at La Spezia.

GARDENIA *Author's Collection*

64. GARDENIA (4) (1945 — 1964) Steel Steamship.
ON. 160733. 4125g, 2463n, 6485d, 364.8 × 51.0 × 24.9 feet.
T. 3-cyl. by North Eastern Marine Engineering Co. Ltd., Newcastle upon Tyne.
7.1930: Completed by Northumberland Shipbuilding Co. (1927) Ltd., Newcastle upon Tyne as BRIARWOOD for Constantine Shipping Co. Ltd., Middlesbrough. *1932:* Transferred to Joseph Constantine S.S. Line Ltd. *1945:* Purchased by Stag Line, Ltd. for £70,468 and renamed GARDENIA. *1947:* Converted from coal to oil burning. *1964:* Sold to Amfitriti Cia. Nav. S.A., Panama for £75,000 and renamed AIS NICOLAS. *1965:* Sold to Astrosplendor Cia. Nav. S.A., Panama. *20.10.1968:* Extensively damaged when fire broke out in the engineroom whilst undergoing repairs at Port Said and declared a total loss. Sold to Adly Makari and broken up at Port Said.

EMPIRE KUMASI *Author's Collection*

65. IXIA (3) (1946 — 1951) Steel Steamship.
ON. 169517. 7201g, 4935n, 9653d, 432.7 × 56.2 × 34.4 feet.
T. 3-cyl. by Fairfield Shipbuilding and Engineering Co. Ltd., Glasgow.
12.1944: Completed by Wm. Hamilton and Co. Ltd., Port Glasgow as EMPIRE KUMASI for the Ministry of War Transport (Joseph Robinson and Sons managers). *1946:* Purchased by Stag Line, Ltd. for £137,000. Converted from coal to oilburning at a cost of £52,479. *1947:* Renamed IXIA. *11.1951:* Sold to Century Shipping Corporation, Liberia for £425,000 and renamed EMPIRE TRADER. *1954:* Sold to Cia. Atlantica Pacifica S.A., Liberia and renamed NORTH RIVER. *1960:* Sold to Italian shipbreakers and *31.1.1960* arrived at Spezia to be broken up by A.R.D.E.M.

IXIA *J. Clarkson*

66. CLINTONIA (5) (1946 — 1959) Steel Steamship.
ON. 168968. 7013g, 4226n, 10170d, 431.0 × 56.2 × 34.2 feet.
T. 3-cyl. by D. Rowan and Co. Ltd., Glasgow.
10.1941: Completed by Lithgows Ltd., Port Glasgow as EMPIRE BAFFIN for the Ministry of War Transport (Joseph Robinson and Sons managers). *1943:* Commissioned by the Admiralty and renamed H.M.S. SANCROFT. Converted for pipelaying duties in connection with the PLUTO (Pipe Line Under The Ocean) operation. *1946:* Purchased by Stag Line, Ltd. for £30,000. Converted back to a drycargo ship and from coal to oil burning at a cost of £137,911. *1947:* Renamed CLINTONIA. *10.12.1959:* Sold to Alcestis Shipping Co. S.A., Greece for £62,500 and renamed ASPIS. *1963:* Sold to Japanese shipbreakers for £14 per light weight ton.

CLINTONIA *Author's Collection*

H.M.S. MORAY FIRTH *Author's Collection*

67. LINARIA (3) (1947 — 1954). Steel Steamship.
ON. 148816. 7333g, 4222n, 10065d, 431.2 × 56.3 × 35.6 feet.
T. 3-cyl. by the Shipbuilders.
10.7.1944: Launched by J. Readhead and Sons Ltd., South Shields as the maintenance ship
H.M.S. MORAY FIRTH for the Admiralty. She had been laid down as EMPIRE PITCAIRN for the
Ministry of War Transport. *12.1947:* Purchased by Stag Line, Ltd. for £80,500. Converted to a
drycargo ship by Tyne Dock Engineering Co. Ltd., South Shields at a cost of £98,597. Renamed
LINARIA. *4.1948:* Commenced trading. *11.1954:* Sold to Chellew Navigation Co. Ltd., London
for £230,000 and renamed ESKGLEN. *1956:* Owners restyled as Esk Shipping Co. Ltd. *1961:*
Sold to Fortune Shipping Co. Ltd., Hong Kong and renamed MARINE FORTUNE. *1961:* Sold to
Herald Shipping Co. Ltd. (World Wide (Shipping) Ltd. managers), Hong Kong. *1967:* Sold to
Japanese shipbreakers and *8.6.1967* arrived at Yokosuka to be broken up.

LINARIA *Skyfotos*

ZINNIA on trials off R. Tyne in 1951 *Author's Collection*

68. ZINNIA (2) (1951 — 1964) Steel Steamship.
ON. 148819. 7292g, 3921n, 10550d, 424.6 × 57.2 × 34.9 feet.
T. 3-cyl. by Dominion Engine Works Ltd., Lachine.
12.1945: Completed by Burrard Dry Dock Co. Ltd., Vancouver as the maintenance and repair ship H.M.S. PORTLAND BILL for the Admiralty. *1.1951:* Purchased by Stag Line, Ltd. for £61,700. Converted to a drycargo ship by Mercantile Dry Dock Co. Ltd., Jarrow on Tyne at a cost of £109,171. Renamed ZINNIA. *18.6.1951:* Commenced trading. *12.1964:* Sold to Astrosuerte Cia. Nav. S.A., Liberia for £63,500 and renamed CHRYSOPOLIS. *1965:* Sold to Formosan (Taiwan) shipbreakers and *18.5.1965* arrived at Kaohsiung to be broken up.

CAMELLIA *Author's Collection*

69. CAMELLIA (4) (1953 — 1972) Steel Motorship.
ON. 148820. 6161g, 3168n, 7800d, 434'6" × 55'8" × 23'7"
4-cyl. 2 S.C.S.A. Doxford oil engine by North Eastern Marine Engineering Co. (1938) Ltd., Wallsend on Tyne.
2.1953: Completed by J. Readhead and Sons Ltd., South Shields for Stag Line, Ltd. Cost £482,136. *6.1972:* Sold to Compania Navegacao Somerset S.A., Panama for £96,000 and renamed GALICIA. *1977:* Sold to Hughes Bolckow Ltd. and *21.4.1977* arrived at Blyth to be broken up.

38

CYDONIA on trials   *Author's Collection*

70. CYDONIA (4) (1955 — 1969) Steel Steamship.
ON. 148822. 6231g, 3219n, 8180d, 433'9" × 57'0" × 24'1"
T. 3-cyl. with low pressure steam turbine by the Shipbuilders.
10.1955: Completed by J. Readhead and Sons Ltd., South Shields for Stag Line, Ltd. Cost
£578,071. *29.8.1969:* Sold to Republic Maritime Corporation, Liberia for U.S.$635,000 and
renamed VERMONT I. *9.1972:* Sold to Renaissance Shipping Co., Liberia and renamed
RENAISSANCE. *1973:* Sold to Cristobal Nav. Corporation, Liberia and renamed SOVEREIGN
EDITH. *1975:* Sold to Anchor Marine Enterprises Ltd., Liberia and renamed JOY. *8.6.1977:* Sank
about 100 miles S.E. of the mouth of the River Mississippi in a position 27.55N. 88.26W. after
three explosions in the engine room. The ship was being towed to New Orleans at the time after
developing rudder trouble whilst on a voyage from Acajutla to New Orleans.

GLOXINIA on trials   *Author's Collection*

71. GLOXINIA (3) (1958 — 1977) Steel Motorship.
ON. 187929. 7665g, 3943n, 10350d, 479'8" × 60'3" × 25'7"
4-cyl. 2 S.C.S.A. Doxford oil engine by North Eastern Marine Engineering Co. Ltd., Wallsend on
Tyne.
5.1958: Completed by J. Readhead and Sons Ltd., South Shields for Stag Line, Ltd. Cost
£958,611. *1.1.1977:* Sold to Panous Shipping Co. Inc., Liberia for U.S.$925,000 and renamed
VIRGINIA M. *30.4.1981:* Sailed from Lagos, with crankshaft damage, in tow of the German tug
LUNEPLATE, 226/65 and *10.6.1981* arrived at Piraeus to be laid up. *7.1982:* Sold to Greek
shipbreakers who commenced demolition *2.8.1982* at Perama.

PHOTINIA   *J. K. Byass*

PHOTINIA as a cable layer   *J. K. Byass*

72. PHOTINIA (3) (1961 — 1978) Steel Motorship.
ON. 187933. 7676g, 3946n, 10340d, 479'8" x 60'3" x 25'7"
4-cyl. 2 S.C.S.A. Doxford oil engine by North Eastern Marine Engineering Co. Ltd., Wallsend on Tyne.
3.1961: Completed by J. Readhead and Sons Ltd., South Shields for Stag Line, Ltd. Cost £919,216. *12.5.1978:* Driven aground at Milwaukee after dragging her anchors in a storm. She was awaiting a berth at Milwaukee after arriving from Chicago. *15.5.1978:* Declared a constructive total loss and abandoned to the underwriters. $1,760,000 (£953,426) paid by insurers. *6.1978:* Sold "as is, as lies" for $5,000 to Selvick Marine Towing Corporation, U.S.A. *7.7.1978:* Refloated with the aid of six tugs and towed to Sturgeon Bay where her machinery was removed. *12.1978:* Towed to Chicago. *15.11.1979:* Arrived in tow at Kewaunee, Wisconsin to be broken up by Baskins Bros.

IXIA   *Author's Collection*

73. IXIA (4) (1964 — 1982) Steel Motorship.
ON. 187944. 15910g, 10237n, 24000d, 595'0" × 75'0" × 32'8"
6-cyl. 2 S.C.S.A. Sulzer oil engine by Geo. Clark and N.E.M. Ltd., Sunderland.
11.1964: Completed by Austin and Pickersgill Ltd., Sunderland for Stag Line, Ltd. Cost
£1,337,575. *5.2.1982:* Sold to Telemachus Shipping Co. S.a.r.l., Lebanon for U.S. $2,850,000
less 3% and renamed TELEMACHUS. Still in service.

ZINNIA *Author's Collection*

74. ZINNIA (3) (1968 — 1982) Steel Motorship.
ON. 187949. 16122g, 10199n, 26603d, 597'0" × 74'9" × 46'4"
6-cyl. 2 S.C.S.A. Sulzer oil engine by Geo. Clark and N.E.M. Ltd., Sunderland.
10.1968: Completed by J. Readhead and Sons Ltd., South Shields for Stag Line, Ltd. Cost
£1,625,552 less £382,119 Government Grant = £1,243,433. *1.11.1982:* Sold to Norbulk Pte.
Ltd. (Thome and Co. Pte. Ltd. managers), Singapore for U.S. $1,750,000 (£1,054,216) and
renamed TIMUR SWIFT. *1983:* Sold to Arm. Ermione S.A., Liberia and renamed ERMIONE. Still
in service.

KIELDER STAG *Skyfotos*

75. KIELDER STAG (1975 — 1978) Steel Motorship.
ON. 364012. 726g, 440n, 1017d, 53.04 × 10.16 × 4.40 metres.
8-cyl. 4 S.C.S.A. oil engine by Naval-Stork-Werkspoor S.A., Cadiz.
9.1969: Completed by Astilleros de Murueta S.A., Murueta as BEGONA DE ASTOBIZA for
Naviera Murueta S.A., Spain. *1.4.1975:* Purchased by Stag Line, Ltd. for £361,075, including
£26,552 to bring her up to British flag requirements, and renamed KIELDER STAG. *1.5.1975:*
Commenced a two year bareboat charter to Kielder Shipping Ltd., Newcastle upon Tyne.
22.1.1976: Bareboat charter ceased on the liquidation of Kielder Shipping Ltd. and management
transferred to G.T. Gillie and Blair Ltd., Newcastle upon Tyne. *20.5.1978:* Sold to Northumbria
Shipping Ltd. (same managers), Newcastle upon Tyne for £300,000 and renamed
NORTHUMBRIA ROSE. Still in service.

SILLOTH STAG   *Skyfotos*

76. SILLOTH STAG (1975 — 1982) Steel Motorship.
ON. 338115. 799g, 435n, 1165d, 57.61 × 10.20 × 4.58 metres.
8-cyl. 4 S.C.S.A. oil engine by W. H. Allen, Sons and Co. Ltd., Bedford.
31.12.1974: Launched by Beverley Shipbuilding and Engineering Co. Ltd., Beverley as
TILSTONE MAID for Tilling Construction Co. Ltd., London. *3.1975:* Completed but not registered.
10.4.1975: Purchased by Stag Line, Ltd. for £585,412 including minor modifications and
renamed SILLOTH STAG. *21.4.1975:* Commenced a four year bareboat charter to Silloth
Shipping Ltd., Annan of which the shareholders were Carrs Milling Industries Ltd., Carlisle, David
Gardiner Securities Ltd., Dumfries and from 11.1975 Stag Line Ltd. *27.5.1982:* Redelivered
from bareboat charter and management transferred to G. T. Gillie and Blair Ltd., Newcastle upon
Tyne. *1.7.1982:* Sold to Westfield Shipping Co. Ltd. which had recently been purchased by
James Fisher and Sons p.l.c., Barrow, G.T. Gillie and Blair Ltd. continued as managers. Still in
service.

BEGONIA   *A. Duncan*

77. BEGONIA (4) (1978 — 1983) Steel Motorship.
ON. 364016. 16329g, 10687n, 26320d, 173.74 × 22.94 × 14.38 metres.
6-cyl. 2 S.C.S.A. Sulzer oil engine by Barclay, Curle and Co. Ltd., Glasgow.
5.1978: Completed by Swan Hunter Shipbuilders Ltd., Walker Shipyard, Newcastle upon Tyne
for Stag Line, Ltd. Cost £7,019,035 assisted by a loan of £4,760,000 under the U.K.
Government Shipbuilding Credit Scheme. *29.3.1983:* Sold to Southbulk Shipping Pte. Ltd.,
Singapore for $4,750,000 (£3,275,682) and renamed TIMUR SWALLOW. Still in service.

SHIPS MANAGED ON BEHALF OF THE GOVERNMENT

M.1. EMPIRE BAFFIN (1941 — 1946) Steel Steamship.
See CLINTONIA (5) (No. 66).

EMPIRE SQUIRE *South Tyneside Museum*

M.2. EMPIRE SQUIRE (1942 — 1943) Steel Steamship.
ON. 168652. 7044g, 4967n, 10400d, 430.9 × 56.2 × 35.2 feet.
T. 3-cyl. by the Shipbuilders.
1.1942: Completed by J. Readhead and Sons Ltd., South Shields for the Ministry of War Transport (Joseph Robinson and Sons managers). *1943:* Transferred to Greek Government (Lyras and Lemos Bros. Ltd. managers) and renamed MAKEDONIA. *1947:* Sold to A.G. Pappadakis, Greece. *1962:* Sold to Cia. Naviera y de Comercio Adonis Ltd., Lebanon and renamed ANTHAS. *1967:* Sold to Chinese shipbreakers.

OCEAN HUNTER nearing completion *Author's Collection*

M.3. OCEAN HUNTER (1942 — 1944) Steel Steamship.
ON. 168639. 7178g, 4280n, 10490d, 421.5 × 57.0 × 34.8 feet.
T. 3-cyl. by John Inglis Co. Ltd., Toronto.
27.9.1942: Launched and *10.1942* completed by Todd-Bath Iron Shipbuilding Corporation, Portland, Maine for the Ministry of War Transport (Joseph Robinson and Sons managers). *10.1.1944:* Torpedoed and sunk by enemy aircraft in a position 36.07N. 0.11E. off the Algerian coast.

M.4. EMPIRE STANDARD (1942 — 1943) Steel Steamship.
ON. 165846. 7047g, 4940n, 10300d, 430.9 × 56.2 × 35.2 feet.
T. 3-cyl. by North Eastern Marine Engineering Co. (1938) Ltd., Newcastle upon Tyne.
10.1942: Completed by Armstrong, Whitworth and Co. (Shipbuilders) Ltd., Newcastle upon Tyne for the Ministry of War Transport (Joseph Robinson and Sons managers). *9.3.1943:* Torpedoed and seriously damaged in a position 36.51N. 01.09E. and taken into Algiers. *26.3.1943:* Bombed and sunk during an air attack on Algiers and abandoned as a total loss.

EMPIRE STANDARD *National Maritime Museum*

EMPIRE HEATH   *National Maritime Museum*

M.5. EMPIRE HEATH (1942 — 1944) Steel Steamship.
ON. 168909. 6643g, 4797n, 9730d, 416.8 × 56.6 × 34.0 feet.
T. 3-cyl. by North Eastern Marine Engineering Co. (1938) Ltd., Sunderland.
1941: Completed by Bartram and Sons Ltd., Sunderland for the Ministry of War Transport (Mark Whitwill and Son Ltd. managers). *1942:* Management transferred to Joseph Robinson and Sons.
11.5.1944: Torpedoed and sunk by the German submarine U.129 in an approximate position 19S. 31W. with the loss of all hands.

M.6. FORT CREVIER (1943 — 1944) Steel Steamship.
ON. 169712. 7131g, 4241n, 10384d, 424.5 × 57.2 × 34.9 feet.
T. 3-cyl. by Dominion Engineering Works Ltd., Montreal.
10.1943: Completed by United Shipyards Ltd., Montreal for the Canadian Government and bareboat chartered to the Ministry of War Transport (Joseph Robinson and Sons managers).
14.4.1944: Seriously damaged whilst at Bombay when the steamer FORT STIKINE, 7142/42 blew up nearby. Subsequently used as a storage hulk. *1948:* Broken up.

M.7. EMPIRE LANKESTER (1944 — 1946) Steel Steamship.
ON. 180071. 7067g, 4844n, 10200d, 431.5 × 56.2 × 35.2 feet.
T. 3-cyl. by Central Marine Engine Works, West Hartlepool.
4.1944: Completed by Wm. Gray and Co. Ltd., West Hartlepool for the Ministry of War Transport (Joseph Robinson and Sons managers). *1946:* Management transferred to Cayzer, Irvine and Co. Ltd. *1948:* Sold to The Clan Line Steamers Ltd. (Cayzer, Irvine and Co. Ltd. managers), Glasgow and renamed CLAN MACKELLAR. *1961:* Sold to Mullion and Co. Ltd., Hong Kong and renamed ARDGROOM. *1967:* Sold to Lee Sing Co. and *20.2.1967* arrived at Hong Kong to be broken up.

EMPIRE LANKESTER   *A. Duncan*

45

SAMADANG at Sydney   *Author's Collection*

M.8. SAMADANG (1944 — 1948) Steel Steamship.
ON. 180493. 7219g, 4380n, 10494d, 422.8 × 57.0 × 34.8 feet.
T. 3-cyl. by Harrisburg Machinery Corporation, Harrisburg.
4.1944: Completed by New England Shipbuilding Corporation, Portland, Maine for the United States War Shipping Administration and bareboat chartered to the Ministry of War Transport (Joseph Robinson and Sons managers). *7.1948:* Returned to United States Maritime Commission and laid up in the U.S. Reserve Fleet. *1968:* Sold to Southern Scrap Material Co. Ltd. and broken up at New Orleans.

M.9. EMPIRE KUMASI (1944 — 1946) Steel Steamship.
See IXIA (3) (No. 65).

SPEED AND FUEL CONSUMPTION

The first steamship in the fleet was the STEPHANOTIS built in 1871. She had a full set of sails and originally had a low powered single expansion two cylinder steam engine. Following ships had two cylinder compound steam engines with provision for sails up to and including the ROBINIA built in 1884. The next ship, the GLOXINIA built in 1897, had a triple expansion steam engine with no provision for sails. Superheating was introduced into the Company's ships during the 1920's.

During the period 1946-1948 the coal burning ships were converted into oil burning, the last coal burner, the CYDONIA built in 1927 was lost during October 1949 when she struck a rogue mine in Cardigan Bay. The CAMELLIA, built in 1953, was the Company's first motorship.

The following table shows increasing speed and consumption over the years.

1871. STEPHANOTIS (1). Sail and 2 cyl. single expansion engine of 98 IHP on 40 lbs steam pressure. About 7.5 knots on about 10 tons of coal.

1875. AMY DORA. Sail and 2 cyl. compound engine of 150 IHP on 70 lbs steam pressure. About 7 knots on about 10 tons of coal.

1876. CYDONIA (1). Sail and 2 cyl. compound engine of 150 IHP on 75 lbs steam pressure. About 7.75 knots on about 11 tons of coal.

1877. AZALEA. Sail and 2 cyl. compound engine of 160 IHP on 75 lbs steam pressure. About 7.9 knots on about $12\frac{1}{4}$ tons of coal.

1879. GARDENIA (1). Sail and 2 cyl. compound engine of 185 IHP. About 8 knots on about $13\frac{1}{4}$ tons of coal.

1884. ROBINIA. Sail and 2 cyl. compound engine. About 8.5 knots on 16 tons of coal.

1920. GLOXINIA (2). Triple expansion engine, 180 lbs superheated steam pressure. About 9 knots on about 21 tons of fuel oil.

1927. CYDONIA (3). Triple expansion engine, 180 lbs superheated steam pressure. About 9 knots on about 18 tons of coal.

1929. PHOTINIA (2). Triple expansion engine, 180 lbs superheated steam pressure. About 8 knots on $22\frac{1}{4}$ tons of coal. After conversion to oil burning about 9.5 knots on 21 tons of fuel oil.

1941. CLINTONIA (5). Triple expansion engine, 220 lbs superheated steam pressure (forced draught). About 10 knots on 26 tons of fuel oil.

1944. LINARIA (3). Triple expansion engine of 2446 IHP on 220 lbs steam pressure. About 10.5 knots on 28 tons of fuel oil.

1953. CAMELLIA (4). 4 cyl. Doxford oil engine of 3,000 BHP. About 12 knots on about 12 tons of diesel oil.

1958. GLOXINIA (3). 4 cyl. Doxford oil engine of 4,400 BHP. (3,282 kw). About 13 knots on about 15 tons of intermediate fuel oil.

1968. ZINNIA (3). 6 cyl. Sulzer R.D.76 oil engine of 9,600 BHP (7,162 kw). About 14 knots on about 30 tons of intermediate fuel oil.

1978. BEGONIA (4). 6 cyl. Sulzer R.N.D.76 oil engine of 12,000 BHP. (8,952 kw) About 14.5 knots on about 31 tons of intermediate fuel oil.

INDEX

ALBERT		5	ELIZABETH MASSEY		63	LINARIA	(1)	49
AMARYLLIS	(1)	22	EMPIRE BAFFIN		M1	LINARIA	(2)	58
AMARYLLIS	(2)	45	EMPIRE HEATH		M5	LINARIA	(3)	67
AMY DORA		21	EMPIRE KUMASI		M9	NUPHAR	(1)	18
AZALEA		25	EMPIRE LANKESTER		M7	NUPHAR	(2)	35
BEGONIA	(1)	42	EMPIRE SQUIRE		M2	NYMPHAEA	(1)	17
BEGONIA	(2)	55	EMPIRE STANDARD		M4	NYMPHAEA	(2)	36
BEGONIA	(3)	63	EUPHORBIA	(1)	46	OCEAN HUNTER		M3
BEGONIA	(4)	77	EUPHORBIA	(2)	54	PHOTINIA	(1)	50
BLESSING		1	EUPHORBIA	(3)	59	PHOTINIA	(2)	62
CADUCEUS		13	FELLOWSHIP		3	PHOTINIA	(3)	72
CAMELLIA	(1)	7	FORT CREVIER		M6	ROBINIA	(1)	24
CAMELLIA	(2)	27	GARDENIA	(1)	30	ROBINIA	(2)	39
CAMELLIA	(3)	52	GARDENIA	(2)	51	ROBINSONS		6
CAMELLIA	(4)	69	GARDENIA	(3)	61	SAMADANG		M8
CLEMATIS		41	GARDENIA	(4)	64	SILLOTH STAG		76
CLINTONIA	(1)	8	GLADIOLUS	(1)	9	STAG	(1)	2
CLINTONIA	(2)	33	GLADIOLUS	(2)	32	STAG	(2)	10
CLINTONIA	(3)	47	GLOXINIA	(1)	40	STAG	(3)	20
CLINTONIA	(4)	53	GLOXINIA	(2)	56	STAG	(4)	37
CLINTONIA	(5)	66	GLOXINIA	(3)	71	STEPHANOTIS	(1)	15
CORONILLA		29	IXIA	(1)	34	STEPHANOTIS	(2)	44
CYDONIA	(1)	23	IXIA	(2)	57	TELEGRAM		14
CYDONIA	(2)	48	IXIA	(3)	65	VIOLA		31
CYDONIA	(3)	60	IXIA	(4)	73	WELLINGTON		16
CYDONIA	(4)	70	JOHN BARING		12	ZINNIA	(1)	43
DANAE		19	KIELDER STAG		75	ZINNIA	(2)	68
EGLANTINE		28	LAURESTINA	(1)	26	ZINNIA	(3)	74
ELEANOR GRACE	(1)	4	LAURESTINA	(2)	38			
ELEANOR GRACE	(2)	11						

ACKNOWLEDGEMENTS

I would like to thank the World Ship Society, its Central Record Team, L. Gray deceased and those who have kindly provided photographs. I would also like to thank Michael Crowdy, Roy Fenton and especially Harold Appleyard for all their work in compiling and editing this fleet list and history.

Nicholas J. Robinson

ISBN 0 905617 30 4

Printed by **Gibbons Barford Print,** Wolverhampton, England